GW00585235

V&A Pattern
Garden Florals

V&A Publishing

V&A Pattern
Garden Florals

First published by V&A Publishing, 2010
V&A Publishing
Victoria and Albert Museum
South Kensington
London SW7 2RL

ISBN 978 1 85177 588 0
Library of Congress Control Number 2009932301

10 9 8 7 6 5 4 3 2 1
2014 2013 2012 2011 2010

A catalogue record for this book is available
from the British Library.

Design: Rose

Front cover (A):
Walter Crane/Jeffrey & Co.
Day Lily, wallpaper. Colour woodblock print on paper.
UK, 1897 (V&A: E.5149–1919)
Pages 2–3 (B):
F. Steiner & Co.
Printed cotton. UK, 1903 (V&A: T.149–1957)
Page 6 (C):
Steiner & Co.
Furnishing fabric. Roller-printed cotton. UK, 1903 (V&A: T.181–1957)
Page 11 (D):
F. Steiner & Co.
Roller-printed cotton. UK, 1902 (V&A: T.163–1957)
Pages 78–9 (E):
Steiner & Co.
Furnishing fabric. Roller-printed cotton. UK, 1906 (V&A: T.183–1957)

Letters (in brackets) refer to the file name of the
images on the accompanying disc.

Printed in China

V&A Publishing
Victoria and Albert Museum
South Kensington
London SW7 2RL
www.vandabooks.com

V&A Pattern

Each *V&A Pattern* book is an introduction to the Victoria and Albert Museum's extraordinarily diverse collection. The museum has more than three million designs for textiles, decorations, wallpapers and prints; some well-known, others less so. This series explores pattern-making in all its forms, across the world and through the centuries. The books are intended to be both beautiful and useful – showing patterns to enjoy in their own right and as inspiration for new design.

V&A Pattern presents the greatest names and styles in design, while also highlighting the work of anonymous draughtsmen and designers, often working unacknowledged in workshops, studios and factories, and responsible for designs of aesthetic originality and technical virtuosity. Many of the most interesting and imaginative designs are seen too rarely. *V&A Pattern* gathers details from our best objects and hidden treasures from pattern books, swatch books, company archives, design records and catalogues to form a fascinating introduction to the variety and beauty of pattern at the V&A.

The compact disc at the back of each book invites you to appreciate the ingenuity of the designs, and the endless possibilities for their application. To use the images professionally, you need permission from V&A Images, as the V&A controls – on behalf of others – the rights held in its books and CD-Roms. *V&A Pattern* can only ever be a tiny selection of the designs available at www.vandaimages.com. We see requests to use images as an opportunity to help us to develop and improve our licensing programme – and for us to let you know about images you may not have found elsewhere.

Garden Florals
Antonia Brodie

The designs for textiles and wallpapers that feature in this book have much in common. They all depict a range of motifs derived from the natural world, most are British, and they date mainly from the period 1880–1910. The majority are printed, although there are also a number of textiles in which pattern is created through weaving, several original watercolour designs for wallpaper, and a splendid hand-printed wallpaper produced by Jeffrey & Co. in 1894 (plate 37).

The scale and colours that are chosen for a given design offer infinite possibilities for changing its appearance. The range of different effects that can be achieved with a single colour is impressive. A simple block design in a strong colour on a contrasting background is bold and arresting while a more closely-patterned design in a subtle colour on a toning background can create shading and texture. The addition of a second colour can intensify both effects. This phenomenon is strikingly illustrated by two examples of the same two-colour designs shown here (plates 1 and 2). The more colours used in a design, the more difficult and expensive it is to produce because, in the case of printed textiles and wallpaper, colours are laid down consecutively. The examples here range from a single colour to a virtuoso eight colour printed textile manufactured by Steiner & Co. in 1902 (see p.11).

Until the 1860s, manufacturers usually employed in-house designers to create their textiles and wallpapers. These designers had the requisite technical knowledge for developing repeating patterns suited to printing or weaving but lacked design education. The educational institutions established after the Great Exhibition of 1851 probably instigated changes that resulted in productive collaborations between artists and manufacturers. A wide range of factors shaped the ways in which these artists chose to depict plant forms: scientific discovery, technological innovation, the expansion of trade, and the rediscovery of art from the past and from different cultures.

The study of botany advanced significantly during the nineteenth century, and increased understanding of the physical make-up of plants and flowers can be seen in art and design. It did not, however, lead to greater naturalism in the depiction of plant forms as designers agreed that these forms should be in some way conventionalised. In the 1840s and 1850s, conventionalised plant motifs manifested themselves as either rigidly geometric two-dimensional forms or painterly renderings. In contrast, later designers, such as William Morris, Walter Crane and C.F.A. Voysey, adapted the forms of plants and creatures to reflect better their natural characteristics.

Included here are William Morris's first designs for wallpaper and printed textiles (plates 25 and 26). Both feature a trellis that provides a geometric framework for naturalistic motifs of flowers and birds. Morris was greatly influenced by the figurative depiction of the natural world in medieval manuscripts and the stylized plant forms and repetitive geometry of Islamic art. This combination of realistically depicted plants and animals in a strong framework, created from stylised leaves and flowers, was crucial to the popularity of Morris's designs and was widely copied.

The accession of Emperor Meiji to the Japanese throne in 1867 opened Japan to trade with Britain for the first time since the introduction of seclusion laws in the 1630s. It led to a flood of Japanese imports, in particular porcelain, lacquer wares, textiles, and woodblock prints. The graphic outlines and dynamic use of colour common to Japanese prints and textiles had a profound influence on the development of the decorative arts in Europe. Aestheticism, Japonisme, and Art Nouveau all incorporated elements derived from Japanese art and design. In particular, motifs such as chrysanthemums, cherry blossoms, sunflowers and peonies became fashionable.

Most nineteenth-century designers adapted natural forms by altering the details and particularities of individual plants and animals to create a simplified but still identifiable motif. Art Nouveau took these simplified motifs and elongated them, creating a sinuous 'whiplash' line, often within a strong geometric structure formed from wavy stems. By the 1920s, this process of adaptation had moved beyond simplification to produce abstract patterns in which plant forms were recognisable as such, but no longer identifiable as botanical specimens.

The 1951 block-printed wallpaper designed by Bent Karlby (plate 66) illustrates one way in which design incorporating plant forms developed. Karlby's design is graphic and two-dimensional and owes much to the tradition of botanical illustration. It shows in naturalistic detail the veins of leaves and their relationship to stems and flowers. It depicts wildflowers – stinging nettle, pignut, corn chamomile, poppies, groundsel, forget-me-not and scarlet pimpernel – that grow in different habitats and flower at different times of year. Despite this anachronistic mix the composition offers a powerful sense of the natural world.

1
Walter Crane/Jeffrey & Co.
Artichoke, wallpaper (see also plate 2). Colour woodblock print on paper. UK, 1895 (V&A: E.5131–1919)

2
Walter Crane/Jeffrey & Co.
Artichoke, wallpaper (see also plate 1). Colour woodblock print on paper. UK, 1895 (V&A: E.5132–1919)

3
Lewis Foreman Day/Jeffrey & Co.
Cactus, wallpaper (see also plate 4). Colour machine print on paper. UK, *c.*1887–1900 (V&A: E.23097–1957)

4
Lewis Foreman Day/Jeffrey & Co.
Cactus, wallpaper (see also plate 3). Colour machine print on paper. UK, *c.*1887–1900 (V&A: E.23098–1957)

5
Lewis Foreman Day/Jeffrey & Co.
Elvas, wallpaper (see also plate 6). Colour machine print on paper. UK, *c*.1887–1900 (V&A: E.23110–1957)

6
Lewis Foreman Day/Jeffrey & Co.
Elvas, wallpaper (see also plate 5). Colour machine print on paper. UK, *c.*1887–1900 (V&A: E.23109–1957)

7
Walter Crane/Jeffrey & Co.
Teazle, wallpaper. Colour woodblock print on paper. UK, 1894 (V&A: E.1839–1934)

8
Lewis Foreman Day/Jeffrey & Co.
Photo, wallpaper. Colour machine print on paper. UK, *c.*1887–1900 (V&A: E.23144–1957)

9
Lewis Foreman Day/Jeffrey & Co.
Athenian, wallpaper. Colour machine print on paper. UK, *c*.1887–1900 (V&A: E.23087–1957)

10
Arthur Silver/The Silver Studio
Woven silk. UK, c.1895 (V&A: CIRC.347–1967)

11
Lewis Foreman Day/Turnbull & Stockdale Ltd
Furnishing fabric. Block-printed cotton. UK, 1888 (V&A: T.16–1954)

12
The Silver Studio
Furnishing fabric. Printed cotton. UK, c.1895 (V&A: T.174:1–1992)

13
C.F.A. Voysey/Essex & Co.
The Oswin, wallpaper. Colour machine print on paper. UK, *c*.1895 (V&A: CIRC.264–1953)

14
John Henry Dearle/Morris & Co./Reprinted by Arthur Sanderson & Sons Ltd
Daffodil, wallpaper. Print on paper. UK, 1880–1917, reprinted *c.*1955 (V&A: E.1419–1979)

15
Charlotte Horne Spiers
Design for a wallpaper. Watercolour and pencil on paper. UK, late 19th century (V&A: E.48–1917)

16
C.F.A. Voysey/Essex & Co.
The Tierney, wallpaper. Colour woodblock print on paper. UK, *c*.1897 (V&A: E.1894–1953)

17
Charles Harrison Townsend/Alexander Morton & Co.
Omar, furnishing fabric. Jacquard-woven wool and cotton double cloth. UK, 1896 (V&A: T.154–1977)

18
The Silver Studio
Furnishing fabric. Woven silk and wool double cloth. UK, c.1900 (V&A: CIRC.280–1966)

19
William Shand Kydd/Shand Kydd Ltd
Ravenna, wallpaper frieze. Outlines block printed and filled in with stencil on paper. UK, 1896 (V&A: E.1524–1954)

20
Arthur Gwatkin/Wyllie & Lochhead Ltd
Flaming Tulip, wallpaper. Machine colour print from engraved rollers on paper. UK, *c.*1901 (V&A: E.467–1967)

21
C.F.A. Voysey/Essex & Co.
Briar, wallpaper. Colour woodblock print on paper. UK, 1901 (V&A: E.1887–1953)

22
Walter Crane/Jeffrey & Co.
Rosamund wallpaper. Colour woodblock print on paper. UK, 1908 (V&A: E.2313–1932)

23
Osborne & Little
Dog Rose, wallpaper. Surflex printed paper. UK, 1979 (V&A: E.445–1986)

24
George Walton / Alexander Morton & Co.
Furnishing fabric. Woven silk and linen. UK, c.1900 (V&A: T.64–1946)

25
William Morris/Morris & Co.
Jasmine Trail, furnishing fabric. Block-printed cotton. UK, 1868–70 (V&A: CIRC.105–1966)

26
William Morris/Morris & Co.
Trellis, wallpaper. Block-printed paper. UK, 1864 (V&A: E.3702–1927)

27
Lindsay P. Butterfield/G.P. & J. Baker
Furnishing fabric. Block-printed linen. UK, c.1900 (V&A: T.59–1953)

28
Harry Napper/The Silver Studio
Kimberley, furnishing fabric. Jacquard woven cotton. UK, c.1902 (V&A: CIRC.250–1966)

29
The Silver Studio/Liberty & Co.
Fabric. Hand-block printed silk. UK, 1897 (V&A: CIRC.233–1966)

30
C.F.A. Voysey
Design for a wallpaper. Ink and watercolour on paper. UK, c.1900 (V&A: E.41–1945)

31
A.H. Lee
Furnishing fabric. Warp-printed woven wool. UK, c.1899 (V&A:T.415–1970)

32
Possibly J. Nicol/Alexander Morton & Co.
Furnishing fabric. Woven silk, wool and cotton double cloth. UK, c.1895 (V&A: T.172–1977)

33
The Silver Studio/G.P.& J. Baker
Hemlock, design for fabric. UK, early 20th century (V&A: E.70–1961)

34
C.F.A. Voysey/Essex & Co.
The Cestrefeld, wallpaper. Colour woodblock print on paper. UK, 1895 (V&A: E.1893–1953)

35
C.F.A. Voysey/Essex & Co.
The Gordon, wallpaper. Colour woodblock print on paper. UK, c.1897 (V&A: E.1898–1953)

36
C.F.A. Voysey / Essex & Co.
The Iolanthe, wallpaper. Colour woodblock print on paper. UK, *c.*1897 (V&A: E.1899–1953)

37
Lewis Foreman Day/Jeffrey & Co.
Como, wallpaper. Colour woodblock print on paper. UK, 1894 (V&A: E.2149–1929)

38
Lindsay P. Butterfield
Design for a woven textile. Watercolour on paper. UK, 1910 (V&A: E.3044–1934)

39
Lewis Foreman Day/Jeffrey & Co.
Sienna, wallpaper (see also plate 40). Colour machine print on paper. UK, *c*.1887–1900 (V&A: E.23158–1957)

40
Lewis Foreman Day/Jeffrey & Co.
Sienna, wallpaper (see also plate 39). Colour machine print on paper. UK, *c*.1887–1900 (V&A: E.23159–1957)

41
Lewis Foreman Day/Wardle & Co.
Furnishing fabric. Block-printed velveteen. UK, c.1888 (V&A: T.81–1953)

42
Osborne & Little Ltd
Illustration of *Throstle* wallpaper design produced by Jeffrey & Co. in 1895. Photo offset. UK, c.1973 (V&A: E.1654A–1974)

43
Charlotte Horne Spiers
Design for a wallpaper. Watercolour and pencil on paper. UK, late 19th century (V&A: E.42–1917)

44
Lindsay P. Butterfield
Furnishing fabric. Roller-printed cotton. UK, c.1895 (V&A: CIRC.665–1966)

45
Walter Crane/Jeffrey & Co.
Francesca, wallpaper. Colour woodblock print on paper. UK, 1902 (V&A: E.1838–1934)

46
Allan Vigars/Jeffrey & Co.
The Rose Bush, wallpaper. Colour woodblock print on paper. UK, 1900 (V&A: E.2230–1913)

47
Walter Crane/Jeffrey & Co.
Dulce Domum, wallpaper. Colour woodblock print on paper. UK, 1904 (V&A: E.5097–1919)

48
Lewis Foreman Day/Turnbull & Stockdale
Furnishing fabric. Roller-printed linen. UK, 1903 (V&A: T.23–1954)

49
Possibly Liberty & Co.
Furnishing fabric. Roller-printed cotton. UK, c.1895 (V&A: CIRC.107–1966)

50
Lindsay P. Butterfield
Design for a cretonne. Watercolour on paper. UK, late 19th century (V&A: E.3055–1934)

51
Charlotte Horne Spiers
Design for a wallpaper. Watercolour on paper. UK, late 19th century (V&A: E.39–1917)

52
Charlotte Horne Spiers
Design for a wallpaper. Watercolour and pencil on paper. UK, late 19th century (V&A: E.46–1917)

53
Walter Crane
Wallpaper. Colour woodblock print on paper. UK, c.1875 (V&A: E.1856–1934)

54
Charlotte Horne Spiers
Design for a wallpaper. Watercolour and pencil on paper. UK, late 19th century (V&A: E.32–1917)

55
Walter Crane/Jeffrey & Co.
Almond Blossom and Swallow, frieze (see also plate 56). Colour woodblock print on paper. UK, 1878 (V&A: E.4037–1915)

56
Walter Crane/Jeffrey & Co.
Wallpaper adapted from *Almond Blossom and Swallow* frieze (see also plate 55). Woodblock print on paper.
UK, *c*.1878 (V&A: E.4021–1915)

57
Walter Crane/Jeffrey & Co.
Day Lily, wallpaper. Colour woodblock print on paper. UK, 1897 (V&A: E.5147–1919)

58
Harry Napper/Alexander Rottmann & Co.
Kingsbury, wallpaper. Colour machine print on paper. UK, *c.*1900 (V&A: E.464–1967)

59
Steiner & Co.
Furnishing fabric. Roller-printed cotton. UK, 1903 (V&A: T.174–1957)

60
Probably the studio of Christopher Dresser/Steiner & Co.
Furnishing fabric. Roller-printed cotton. UK, 1899 (V&A: T.131–1957)

61
Lindsay P. Butterfield
Textile design. Watercolour. UK, 1902 (V&A: E.736–1974)

62
Lindsay P. Butterfield
Textile or wallpaper design. Watercolour and pencil. UK, 1903 (V&A: E.749–1974)

63
C.F.A. Voysey/Essex & Co.
The Nure, wallpaper. Colour woodblock print on paper. UK, *c.*1899 (V&A: E.1885–1953)

64
Lewis Foreman Day/Jeffrey & Co.
Memphis, wallpaper. Colour machine print on paper. UK, c.1887–1900 (V&A: E.23131–1957)

65
Steiner & Co.
Furnishing fabric. Printed cotton. UK, 1902 (V&A: T.144–1957)

66
Bent Karlby/Dahls Tapetfabrik
Haelderne, wallpaper. Colour woodblock print on paper. Denmark, 1951 (V&A: E.897–1979)

Further Reading

Hoskins, Lesley, ed.
*The Papered Wall:
The History, Patterns and
Techniques of Wallpaper*
London, new edition 2005

Hoskins, Lesley and Turner, Mark
*Silver Studio of Design:
A Design and Source Book for
Home Decoration*
Exeter, 1988

Livingstone, Karen and Parry,
Linda, eds.
International Arts and Crafts
London, 2005

Oman, Charles C. and
Hamilton, Jean
*Wallpapers: A History and
Illustrated Catalogue of the
Collection of the Victoria and
Albert Museum*
London, 1982

Parry, Linda
British Textiles from 1850 to 1900
London, 1993

Parry, Linda
*Textiles of the Arts and
Crafts Movement*
London, new edition 2005

Saunders, Gill
Wallpaper in Interior Decoration
London, 2002

Snodin, Michael and Styles, John
*Design and the Decorative Arts:
Britain 1500–1900*
London, 2001